Australian Animals

Tasmanian Devils

ABDO
Publishing Company

Big Buddy BOOKS
Australian Animals

by Julie Murray

VISIT US AT
www.abdopublishing.com

Published by ABDO Publishing Company, 8000 West 78th Street, Edina, Minnesota 55439.

Copyright © 2012 by Abdo Consulting Group, Inc. International copyrights reserved in all countries. No part of this book may be reproduced in any form without written permission from the publisher. Big Buddy Books™ is a trademark and logo of ABDO Publishing Company.

Printed in the United States of America, North Mankato, Minnesota.
052011
092011

♻ PRINTED ON RECYCLED PAPER

Coordinating Series Editor: Rochelle Baltzer
Editor: Marcia Zappa
Contributing Editors: Megan M. Gunderson, BreAnn Rumsch, Sarah Tieck
Graphic Design: Maria Hosley
Cover Photograph: *iStockphoto*: ©iStockphoto.com/auswild.
Interior Photographs/Illustrations: *AnimalsAnimals-Earth Scenes*: ©Prenzel, Fritz (p. 25); *Fairfax Photos*: Nick Moir/Fairfax Photos/The Sydney Morning Herald (p. 23); *Getty Images*: Steve Morenos/Newspix (p. 11), PETER PARKS/AFP (p. 25), Adam Pretty (p. 29), Visuals Unlimited, Inc./Dave Watts (p. 19), Ian Waldie (p. 9); *iStockphoto*: ©iStockphoto.com/davidf (p. 8), ©iStockphoto.com/gprentice (p. 9), ©iStockphoto.com/Matejay (p. 4), ©iStockphoto.com/renelo (p. 11), ©iStockphoto.com/TimothyBall (p. 4); *Photolibrary*: Bios (p. 21), Oxford Scientific (OSF) (p. 15); *Shutterstock*: John Carnemolla (p. 7), Susan Flashman (p. 27), Patsy A. Jacks (pp. 5, 17), Ralph Loesche (p. 27), markhiggins (p. 13).

Library of Congress Cataloging-in-Publication Data

Murray, Julie, 1969-
  Tasmanian devils / Julie Murray.
     p. cm. -- (Australian animals)
  ISBN 978-1-61783-014-3
  1. Tasmanian devil--Juvenile literature. I. Title.
  QL737.M33M87 2012
  599.2'7--dc22
                    2011002303

Contents

Amazing Australian Animals 4

Tasmanian Devil Territory 6

Welcome to the Continent Down Under! 8

Take a Closer Look 10

A Day in the Life 12

Devilish Behavior 14

Mealtime 18

Baby Devils 22

Survivors 26

Crikey! I'll bet you never knew... 30

Important Words 31

Web Sites 31

Index 32

Long ago, nearly all land on Earth was one big mass. About 200 million years ago, the land began to break into **continents**. One of these is an island called Australia.

A Tasmanian devil is about the size of a small dog.

Living on an island allowed Australian animals to **develop** separately from other animals. So today, many are unlike animals found anywhere else in the world! One of these animals is the Tasmanian devil.

Tasmanian Devil Territory

Tasmanian devils live only on Tasmania. This island is a state in the country of Australia. Devils are found all over the island. But, they are most common in the north, east, and center.

Tasmanian devils often live in forests, coastal **scrublands**, and farmlands. They like areas with thick, low plants.

NORTHERN TERRITORY

QUEENSLAND

WESTERN AUSTRALIA

SOUTH AUSTRALIA

NEW SOUTH WALES

VICTORIA

Tasmanian Devil Territory

TASMANIA

Thick, low plants make good hiding spots.

Welcome to the Continent Down Under!

If you took a trip to where Tasmanian devils live, you might find…

…the Bass Strait.

The Bass Strait separates the island of Tasmania from Australia's mainland. It is about 150 miles (240 km) wide. It is north of Tasmania.

INDIAN

West-Australian Basin

North West Cape

Geraldton
Mount Meharry

Perth
Kalgoorlie

Cape Naturaliste
Bunbury
Norseman
Great

Cape Leeuwin
Albany
Arch of the Recherche

Cocos Islands

Christmas

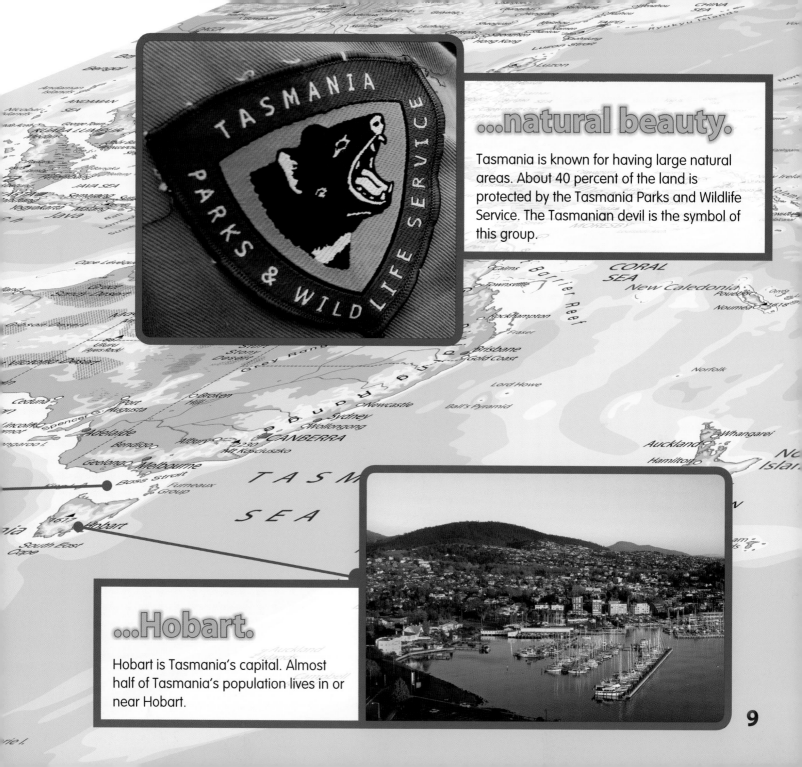

...natural beauty.

Tasmania is known for having large natural areas. About 40 percent of the land is protected by the Tasmania Parks and Wildlife Service. The Tasmanian devil is the symbol of this group.

...Hobart.

Hobart is Tasmania's capital. Almost half of Tasmania's population lives in or near Hobart.

Take a Closer Look

Tasmanian devils have short, sturdy bodies and legs. They have large heads with big ears. Their mouths are lined with big, sharp teeth.

Tasmanian devils have dark brown or black fur. Many have white marks on their chests, sides, and rears.

A Tasmanian devil's size depends on where it lives and what it eats. Most devils are about one foot (0.3 m) tall and two feet (0.6 m) long. They weigh 10 to 25 pounds (5 to 11 kg).

A Tasmanian devil's tail can add up to one foot (0.3 m) of length.

A Tasmanian devil's ears change color when it's scared, excited, or angry. They turn from pale pink to bright red!

Uncovered!

A Tasmanian devil's short legs make it a slow mover. But when in danger, a devil can run quicker by moving both back legs together.

A Day in the Life

Tasmanian devils sleep during the day. They lie in hidden places. These include hollow logs, caves, thick bushes, or underground homes left by other animals.

Most Tasmanian devils live alone. They stay in certain home areas. But, their home areas often include shared land. And, they often come together to feed.

Feeding as a group helps Tasmanian devils tear apart food.

Devilish Behavior

Tasmanian devils are known for the wild ways they **communicate**. They screech and growl loudly. They may show their teeth or dive forward. They do this when scared, fighting for a **mate**, or feeding as a group.

Uncovered!
Tasmanian devils got their name from early European settlers. They called them devils because of their dark color, wild displays, and scary noises.

To get the most food,
Tasmanian devils try to
prove who is most powerful.

Tasmanian devils also **communicate** by yawning and sneezing. Sharp teeth make a devil's yawn look angry. But, usually it means the animal is scared. A sneeze dares another devil to fight!

Uncovered!

A strong sneeze can make a Tasmanian devil look powerful. It can make another back away from a fight.

A yawning Tasmanian devil shows all its teeth!

Mealtime

Tasmanian devils are carnivores (KAHR-nuh-vawrs). That means they eat meat. Devils often eat animals that are already dead. But, they also hunt small animals such as snakes, birds, fish, and insects.

Uncovered!
Tasmanian devils have no natural predators.

Even though Tasmanian devils often eat together, they hunt alone. A devil can hunt large animals, such as wombats. A wombat can weigh up to 80 pounds (36 kg)!

Tasmanian devils feed at night. They may travel as far as ten miles (16 km) searching for food. Devils use their long, **sensitive** whiskers to feel objects in their path. And, they use their strong senses of hearing and smell to find food.

When a Tasmanian devil finds food, it eats as much as it can. Its strong mouth and teeth let it eat all of an animal. That includes the bones and fur!

When food is plentiful, a devil stores fat in its tail. The healthiest devils often have the fattest tails.

A Tasmanian devil's teeth are very close together. This helps them crush bone.

Baby Devils

Tasmanian devils are part of a group of **mammals** called marsupials (mahr-SOO-pee-uhls). Marsupials have tiny babies called joeys.

Joeys are born before they are done **developing**. A newborn joey lives inside a special pouch on its mother's belly. There, it keeps growing.

Tasmanian devil joeys grow quickly. At birth, they are as small as a grain of rice.

Female Tasmanian devils give birth to up to 50 joeys at a time. Newborn joeys crawl in their mother's pouch. But, a mother can only feed up to four joeys at a time. So, only a few **survive**.

After about four months, Tasmanian devil joeys come out of their mother's pouch. They return often to feed. Joeys start eating meat at about six months old. At about eight months old, they are ready to live on their own.

Uncovered!
Young Tasmanian devils can climb trees! Their light bodies and sharp claws make them good climbers. But as they become older, they lose this skill.

Sometimes, mother Tasmanian devils leave joeys in a hidden place while they find food (*above*). Other times, they carry joeys on their backs (*right*).

Survivors

Over the years, Tasmanian devils have faced many dangers. Long ago, farmers killed them to keep their animals safe. Today, devils can be attacked by dogs or hit by cars.

Since the 1990s, Tasmanian devils have faced an even bigger danger. Devil Facial Tumor Disease (DFTD) is a type of cancer. It has killed tens of thousands of Tasmanian devils.

Uncovered!
DFTD causes large bumps on a devil's head and mouth. This makes it hard for the devil to eat. In time, it dies.

DFTD spreads between devils when they bite each other.

Tasmanian devils are endangered. This means they could die out.

27

Still, Tasmanian devils **survive**. Many scientists work with the Australian government to save Tasmanian devils. These special animals help make Australia an amazing place.

Uncovered!
In the wild, Tasmanian devils live five to eight years.

Scientists work to control DFTD. They try to keep healthy devils away from sick ones.

29

Crikey!
I'll bet you never knew...

...that Tasmanian devils are the vacuum cleaners of the forest. They eat just about any dead animal, no matter how old or rotten! This helps keep their home areas clean.

...that the older a Tasmanian devil is, the bigger its head is. A devil's head continues to grow after its body has stopped growing.

...that Tasmanian devils stink! They don't smell all the time. But, they let out a gross odor when worried or bothered.

Important Words

cancer any of a group of very harmful diseases that cause a body's cells to become unhealthy.

communicate (kuh-MYOO-nuh-kayt) to share knowledge, thoughts, or feelings.

continent one of Earth's seven main land areas.

develop to go through steps of natural growth.

mammal a member of a group of living beings. Mammals have hair or fur and make milk to feed their babies.

mate a partner to join with in order to reproduce, or have babies.

scrubland land covered with thick, small bushes and trees.

sensitive able to quickly and easily feel or notice.

survive to continue to live or exist.

Web Sites

To learn more about Tasmanian devils, visit ABDO Publishing Company online. Web sites about Tasmanian devils are featured on our Book Links page. These links are routinely monitored and updated to provide the most current information available.

www.abdopublishing.com

Index

Australia **4, 5, 6, 7, 8, 28**

Bass Strait **8**

body **10, 11, 20, 21, 22, 24, 25, 26, 30**

communication **14, 16, 17**

dangers **11, 26, 27**

Devil Facial Tumor Disease **26, 27, 29**

dingoes **7**

eating habits **10, 12, 13, 14, 15, 18, 19, 20, 21, 24, 25, 30**

fur **10**

habitat **5, 6, 7, 10, 12, 30**

joeys **22, 23, 24, 25**

mammals **22**

marsupials **22**

mating **14**

size **5, 10, 23**

Tasmania **6, 8, 9**

Tasmania Parks and Wildlife Service **9**

teeth **10, 14, 16, 17, 20, 21**